Peace Joy Happiness

Empowerment, An Adult Coloring Book

by Starlene D. Stewart

Peace Joy Happiness : Empowerment, An Adult Coloring Book

ISBN: 978-1-944432-00-3

Front Cover Image: "Happiness" Created and colored by Starlene D. Stewart

Front Cover Design: Starlene D. Stewart

Fonts: Clear Sans, Alex Brush

Copyright © 2015 Starlene D. Stewart

Please do not steal! No part of this book may be copied or sold or used for any other purpose without express written permission from the author. Please do not share this book electronically or on any website or blog.

All rights reserved worldwide. This document is protected by copyright laws.

Published by HQ Productions

http://www.starlene.com

Produced in USA

Table of Contents

How to Use This Book 1

Amazing 3

Awesome 5

Better 7

Blossom 9

Bravery 11

Brilliance 13

Calm 15

Centered 17

Confident 19

Determination 21

Dynamic 23

Energetic 25

Fortitude 27

Gratitude 29

Happiness 31

Harmonious 33

Health 35

Inspire 37

Invincible 39

Joy 41

Jubilant 43

Knowledge 45

Love 47

Motivate	49
Nurtured	51
Optimist	53
Peace	55
Positive	57
Powerful	59
Rejuvenated	61
Serene	63
Tranquil	65
Transform	67
Uplift	69
Victorious	71
Worthy	73
Zippy	75
About the Author	77
Find Starlene Online	78
Other Books by Starlene D. Stewart	79

How to Use This Book

Do you remember coloring as a child? I have many fond memories. I can clearly recall the stack of coloring books Mother kept on the top shelf of her bedroom closet. On certain days she would pull the coloring books down and let my sisters and me choose which ones we would color in. Sometimes it would be pouring rain outside. Or maybe it was during summer break and it was just too hot to be outside in the Arizona summer. Many times she would sit and color with us.

The coloring books of my childhood were thick, the paper coarse, the images detailed. Some even told a story. The only crayons were Crayola™ crayons, and to this day I describe colors using their names[1]... Cornflower blue. Carnation pink. Sea green. Burnt sienna. Sunset orange. Bittersweet. Canary. What about you?

Coloring is how many of us learned the joy of arts and crafting. Some were passionate and grew up to color and paint and make art every day as professional artists, but most of us put down the crayons and other art forms for other activities. Some of us haven't considered coloring in decades. I know I hadn't colored since my boys were little so we're talking almost two decades for me.

You're probably wondering why you would want to color.[2] Well, what is your life like nowadays? Hectic? Crazy-making? Are you busy raising a family? Are you trying to heal from an illness or do you experience anxiety or depression? Are you looking for ways to relax and mellow out? Coloring is making a comeback for adults[3].

Adult coloring books are not your children's coloring books. They are usually theme based and filled with beautiful complex designs. Most adults who color invest in fine-tipped felt markers, colored pencils, or gel pens, since the designs often have very small spaces to fill.

In this book I have created kaleidoscopic designs and matched each one with an empowering word along with its definition. As you color, think on the word and the meaning. What does it represent to you? Why did you choose this word's image to color right now? Bear in mind that these images are not meant to be colored in one sitting! Think of it like putting a jigsaw puzzle together with no chance for losing pieces!

---

[1] Wikipedia. List of Crayola crayon colors. Retrieved September 7, 2015 from https://en.wikipedia.org/wiki/List_of_Crayola_crayon_colors

[2] Fox News. Health Benefits of coloring books attracting adults to childhood pastime. (July 30, 2015). Retrieved September 7, 2015 from http://www.foxnews.com/health/2015/07/30/health-benefits-coloring-books-attracting-adults-to-childhood-pastime/

[3] The Pencentral. Benefits of Coloring Books for Adults. Retrieved September 7, 2015 from http://www.thepencentral.com/view/articles/benefits-of-coloring-books-for-adults-500

Be honest. Isn't it true that when you have some down time you reach for your phone or tablet, sit at the computer or watch television. Maybe you're "farming" or "crushing candy." Shooting invaders or binge-watching a series. Depending on what you're watching or playing, these activities can ramp us up, working against our desire to relax and calm down. If you're doing that before bedtime, it's definitely not conducive to relaxation and sleeping. Recent studies tell us that the lighting from our phones, tablets, and television screens keeps us awake instead of helping us get to sleep[4]. Perhaps you are looking for a new bedtime routine. What about coloring for just ten minutes every evening? Or maybe you will start out your mornings coloring?

My intent in creating this book and these designs was to give adults who are on a healing journey a book to color while concentrating on strong words. Words like Peace, Joy, Happiness, Nurtured, Harmonious... As you color, empower yourself by thinking peaceful, joyous and happy thoughts. Even if you are happy and healthy, you will enjoy relaxing and coloring.

In this book you'll find thirty-five kaleidoscopic designs to color. Choose your design, pick your medium. Are you going to use felt tipped pens, gel pens, crayons, paints? If you have children, some of the designs are simple enough for even young children to color.

I wish you joyful happy coloring!

Starlene

---

[4] Huffington Post. (December 31, 2014). http://www.huffingtonpost.com/2014/12/23/reading-before-bed_n_6372828.html

Amazing

adjective: causing great surprise or wonder

Peace Joy Happiness: Empowerment, An Adult Coloring Book

Awesome

adjective: causing feelings of awe; extremely good

Peace Joy Happiness: Empowerment, An Adult Coloring Book

Better

adjective: improved in health or mental attitude

Peace Joy Happiness: Empowerment, An Adult Coloring Book

Blossom

noun: a peak period or stage of development

Peace Joy Happiness: Empowerment, An Adult Coloring Book

Bravery

noun: the quality or state of being brave; courage

Peace Joy Happiness: Empowerment, An Adult Coloring Book

Brilliance

noun: the quality or state of being brilliant

Peace Joy Happiness: Empowerment, An Adult Coloring Book

Calm

noun: a state of tranquility

Peace Joy Happiness: Empowerment, An Adult Coloring Book

Centered

adjective: emotionally stable and secure

Peace Joy Happiness: Empowerment, An Adult Coloring Book

Peace Joy Happiness: Empowerment, An Adult Coloring Book

Confident

adjective: full of conviction; certain, having or showing assurance and self-reliance

Peace Joy Happiness: Empowerment, An Adult Coloring Book

Determination

noun: the act of deciding definitely and firmly

Peace Joy Happiness: Empowerment, An Adult Coloring Book

Dynamic

adjective: having or showing a lot of energy

Peace Joy Happiness: Empowerment, An Adult Coloring Book

Energetic

adjective: possessing or exhibiting energy, especially in abundance; vigorous

Peace Joy Happiness: Empowerment, An Adult Coloring Book

Fortitude

noun: mental and emotional strength in facing difficulty and adversity

Peace Joy Happiness: Empowerment, An Adult Coloring Book

Gratitude

noun: the quality or feeling of being grateful or thankful

Peace Joy Happiness: Empowerment, An Adult Coloring Book

Happiness

noun: the quality or state of being happy; good fortune; pleasure; contentment; joy

Peace Joy Happiness: Empowerment, An Adult Coloring Book

Harmonious

adjective: forming a pleasantly consistent whole; congruous

Peace Joy Happiness: Empowerment, An Adult Coloring Book

Peace Joy Happiness: Empowerment, An Adult Coloring Book

Health

noun: soundness of body or mind; freedom from disease or ailment

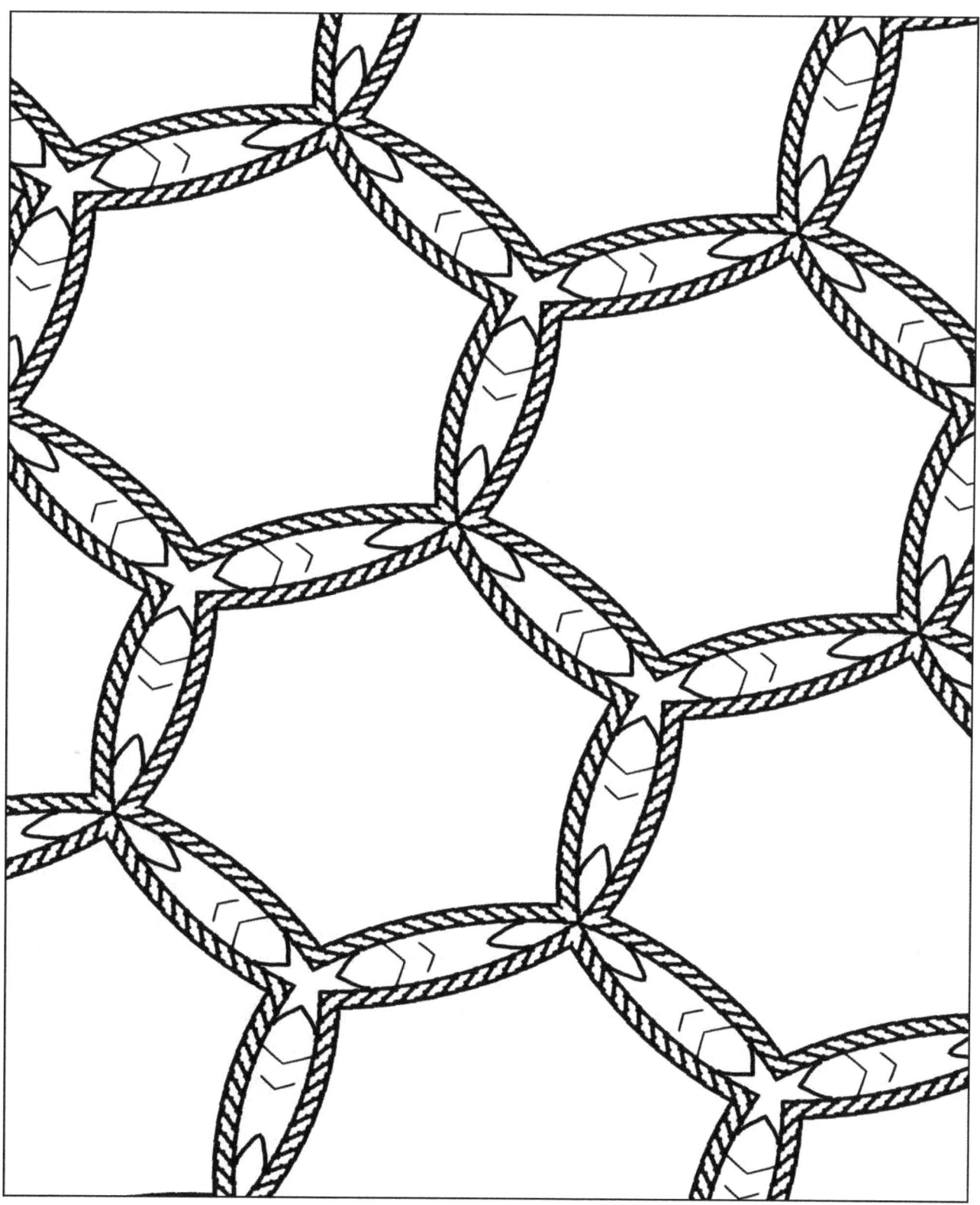

Peace Joy Happiness: Empowerment, An Adult Coloring Book

Inspire

verb: to animate, as an influence, feeling thought or the like

Peace Joy Happiness: Empowerment, An Adult Coloring Book

Invincible

adjective: incapable of being conquered; insurmountable

Peace Joy Happiness: Empowerment, An Adult Coloring Book

Joy

noun: the emotion of great delight or happiness caused by something exceptionally good or satisfying; keen pleasure; elation

Peace Joy Happiness: Empowerment, An Adult Coloring Book

Jubilant

adjective: showing great joy, satisfaction, or triumph; rejoicing; exultant

Peace Joy Happiness: Empowerment, An Adult Coloring Book

Knowledge

noun: the fact or state of knowing; the perception of fact or truth; clear and certain mental apprehension

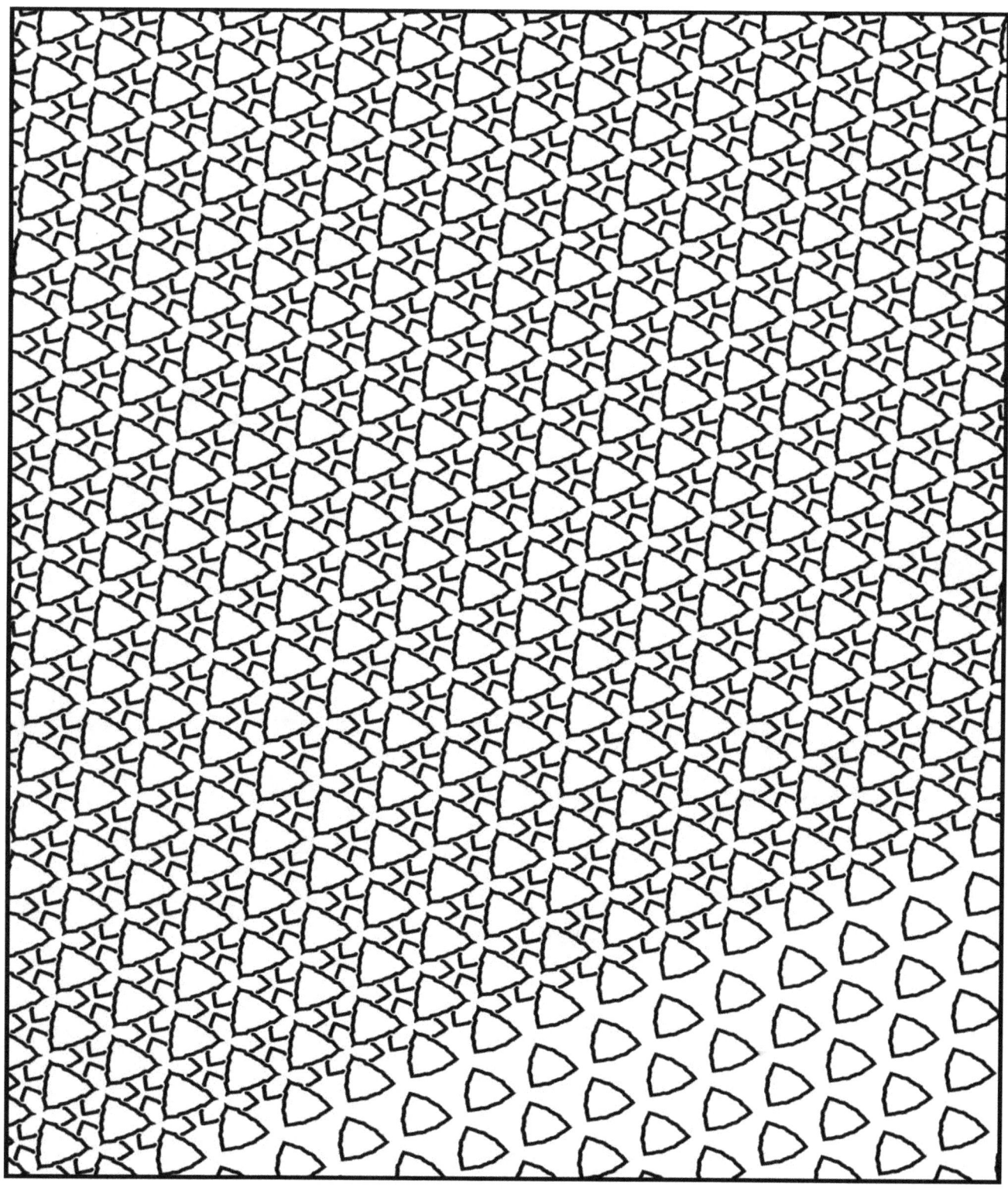

Peace Joy Happiness: Empowerment, An Adult Coloring Book

Love

noun: a profoundly tender, passionate affection for another person

Peace Joy Happiness: Empowerment, An Adult Coloring Book

Motivate

verb: to provide with motive or motives; incite; impel

Peace Joy Happiness: Empowerment, An Adult Coloring Book

Nurtured

verb: to support and encourage, foster

Peace Joy Happiness: Empowerment, An Adult Coloring Book

Optimist

noun: a person who holds the belief or doctrine of optimism

Peace Joy Happiness: Empowerment, An Adult Coloring Book

Peace

noun: freedom of the mind from annoyance; tranquility, serenity

Peace Joy Happiness: Empowerment, An Adult Coloring Book

Positive

adjective: confident in opinion or assertion; fully assured

Peace Joy Happiness: Empowerment, An Adult Coloring Book

Peace Joy Happiness: Empowerment, An Adult Coloring Book

Powerful

adjective: having or exerting great power or force; potent, efficacious

Peace Joy Happiness: Empowerment, An Adult Coloring Book

Rejuvenated

verb: to restore to former state; make fresh or new again

Peace Joy Happiness: Empowerment, An Adult Coloring Book

Serene

adjective: calm, peaceful, or tranquil; unruffled; clear; fair

Peace Joy Happiness: Empowerment, An Adult Coloring Book

Tranquil

adjective: free from commotion or tumult; peaceful; quiet; calm

Peace Joy Happiness: Empowerment, An Adult Coloring Book

Transform

verb: to change in condition, nature, or character; convert

Peace Joy Happiness: Empowerment, An Adult Coloring Book

Uplift

verb: to lift up; raise; elevate; to exalt emotionally or spiritually

Peace Joy Happiness: Empowerment, An Adult Coloring Book

Victorious

adjective: having achieved a victory; conquering, triumphant

Peace Joy Happiness: Empowerment, An Adult Coloring Book

Worthy

adjective: having adequate or great merit, character, or value

Peace Joy Happiness: Empowerment, An Adult Coloring Book

Zippy

adjective: full of zip, very speedy or quick, strikingly fresh, lively or appealing in style

About the Author

Starlene Stewart blogs at GAPS Diet Journey to chronicle her experience on the GAPS™ Diet founded by Dr. Natasha Campbell-McBride. Eating real food and cutting out grains and fake foods made a huge impact on her health. She is always looking for new healing modalities and coloring is one of the newest!

I would love to hear from you! If you have any comments, feedback, questions or just want to reach out, please feel free to send an email to: starlene@gapsdietjourney.com *~Starlene*

Peace Joy Happiness: Empowerment, An Adult Coloring Book

Find Starlene Online

Starlene's Amazon Author Page: http://amazon.com/author/starlene

Starlene's blog: http://www.gapsdietjourney.com

Facebook: http://www.facebook.com/gapsdietjourney
Twitter: http://www.twitter.com/gapsjourney
YouTube: http://www.youtube.com/conscioustar
Pinterest: http://www.pinterest.com/conscioustar
Blog Talk Radio: http://www.blogtalkradio.com/gapsjourney

Sign up for the Baking with Coconut Flour newsletter for announcements:

http://forms.aweber.com/form/67/1760263067.htm

Other Books by Starlene D. Stewart

Visit http://www.starlene.com to learn more

Beyond Grain & Dairy (PDF) contains 113 delicious recipes to tantalize your taste buds, made with no grains, gluten, dairy, gums, corn, soy, or sugar. Go beyond grain and dairy and you may feel better than you have in years!

Mastering the Art of Baking with Coconut Flour (PDF and Amazon Kindle) In this e-book I will teach you about coconut flour, where to find it, how to make sure your recipes turn out successfully, and how to convert wheat flour recipes. I walk you step by step through four recipes to demonstrate the process I take to convert recipes. You can be successful baking with coconut flour and I will show you how!

Everyone Loves Pudding (PDF and Amazon Kindle) is a book of delicious uncooked (raw) puddings that do not include grains, gluten, dairy, gums, corn, soy, or sugar. You'll find flavors like Cherry Vanilla, Creamy Pumpkin, Silky Chocolate, Smooth Lemon, and Apple Raisin. You *can* have super smooth and creamy pudding again, made from real food, dairy-free, creamy, and delicious!

Winter Soups Community Cookbook (PDF) is a collection of 52 soups from real food bloggers. Starlene's Crock Pot Spaghetti Sauce Soup is included along with gorgeous photos for every winter soup.

Naturally Sweetened Treats Community Cookbook (PDF) is a collection of 41 sweet treat dessert recipes from real food bloggers. Starlene's Silky Chocolate Pie is included along with beautiful photos for all of the real food naturally sweetened treats.

Gluten-Free Snacks Community Cookbook (PDF) is a collection of 34 gluten-free snack recipes from real food bloggers. From Appetizers to Crunchy Snacks, No Bake Sweets, and Dips, this e-book is a great place to start if you are gluten-free. Starlene's Pumpkin Poppers are included along with beautiful photos for each real food gluten-free snacks.

Baker's Dozen Sweet Quick Breads (PDF and Amazon Kindle) is Volume 1 in the Coconut Flour Baked Goods series and includes 13 sweet quick bread recipes ranging from well loved favorites like Banana and Lemon Poppy Seed to new creations like Spiced Blackberry and Peanut Butter Chocolate Chunk.

Baker's Dozen Pumpkin Treats (PDF and Amazon Kindle) is Volume 2 in the Coconut Flour Baked Goods series and includes 13 coconut flour baked goods recipes plus 8 other recipes featuring the star of fall, pumpkin! Enjoy waffles, loaves of bread, pudding, non-dairy cheesecake and pumpkin drinks, too.

Baker's Dozen Holiday Quick Breads (PDF and Amazon Kindle) is Volume 3 in the Coconut Flour Baked Goods series and includes 13 coconut flour bread recipes with a focus on traditional holiday breads.

Upcoming Titles from Starlene D. Stewart

Coming in December 2015! **Baker's Dozen Chocolate Treats Volume 4 in the Coconut Flour Baked Goods series will include 13 loaves of chocolate bread plus additional chocolate recipes will be included**.

In 2016 Starlene plans to release several more volumes in the Baker's Dozen Coconut Flour Baked Goods series to include savory quick breads, a second volume of sweet quick breads, a second volume of pumpkin treats and several others.

www.ingramcontent.com/pod-product-compliance
Lightning Source LLC
Chambersburg PA
CBHW081018040426
42444CB00014B/3262